18 Holes of Golf

Written & Illustrated By:
Hillary Scaletta

ISBN: 1539466884
ISBN 13: 9781539466888

For Pa

18 Holes of Golf

By:Hillary Scaletta

Hole Number One!

Let's shoot par. "Par" is the number of strokes you should get on a hole.

Hole Number Two!

Birdie Time! "Birdie" is one under par.

Hole Number
Three!

Let's get an eagle. An "eagle" is two
under par. That's soaring!

Hole Number Four!

It's called a "bogey" when you get one stroke over par.

Hole Number Seven!

"HOLE-IN-ONE!!!"
You'll never forget it!

Hole Number Eight!
Pull out your driver. The
"driver" is the tallest club
in your bag that will help
you hit the ball the
farthest.

Hole Number Nine!

Chip it onto the green. Use a pitching wedge to land the ball onto the green. The "green" is where the hole is located.

Hole Number Ten!

Make sure to hit the ball onto the fairway. The "fairway" is the short grass leading to the "green."

Hole Number Eleven!

Don't forget to keep your head down when you're swinging. It'll help you hit the ball straight.

Hole Number Twelve!

Use your irons once you've made it onto the fairway. The "irons" are the clubs with the numbers 4,5,6,7,8 or 9 on them. Try to lay it up before, or even onto, the green.

Hole Number Thirteen!

Watch out for the ducks on the pond. It's an extra stroke if you land in the water.

Hole Number Fourteen!

When the ball reaches the green, pull out your putter. You'll use the putter to tap the ball into the hole. The "putter" is the smallest club in your bag.

Hole Number Fifteen!

Make sure to bring class to the golf course! Collared shirts, skirts and belts are always welcomed!

Hole Number Sixteen!

Oh No! You hit the ball into the sand. Take out your "sand wedge." Don't touch the sand with your club. That'll cost you a penalty stroke.

Hole Number Eighteen!

We made it! Don't forget
to have fun and swing
easy!

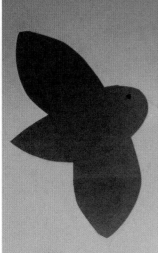

About the Author:

Hillary Scaletta grew up playing golf. Her Pa taught her the game of golf. "He had great patience and you could tell he loved the game." That's why Hillary was encouraged to play. In 2016, Hillary graduated from the University of Redlands, with a degree in Creative Writing. She continues to golf and write.

Made in the USA
Monee, IL
01 March 2022

92066767R00019